CW01638514

Aleph Bet

Sue Rose

For Jacqui

With warm wishes

Sue

Cinnamon Press
:: small miracles from distinctive voices ::

Published by Cinnamon Press
www.cinnamonpress.com

ISBN 978-1-78864-176-0

British Library Cataloguing in Publication Data. A CIP record for this book can be obtained from the British Library.

Designed and typeset in Bodini and FrankRuehl by Cinnamon Press. Cover design by Adam Craig © Adam Craig.

In the EU, we are fully compliant with GPSR (General Product Safety Regulation). Our EU GPSR Authorised Representative, via Inpress Books, is LOGOS EUROPE, 9 rue Nicolas Poussin, 17000, LA ROCHELLE, France E-mail: Contact@logoseurope.eu

Cinnamon Press is represented by Inpress.

Acknowledgements

Acknowledgements are due to the editors of the publications where some of these poems first appeared: *And Other Poems*, *London Grip*, *Minyan*, *Thin Places & Sacred Spaces*, ed. Sarah Law (Amethyst Press).

My deepest thanks to Anne Berkeley, Claire Crowther, Rhona McAdam and Tamar Yoseloff who provided invaluable critical input and encouragement every step of the way, as well as to Geraldine Paine and Robert Stein for their feedback. My lasting gratitude, too, to Rabbi Aaron Goldstein, without whose patient teachings this book would not have been written.

Contents

Preface

I didn't learn Hebrew when I was a small child. By the time I decided to try, I was about ten and the beginner's class was full of very young children. Feeling too cool for *schul*, I stopped going and, indeed, there was no real reason to learn the language as we didn't observe the religious holidays, except Passover, or keep kosher or go to synagogue—my father, who had been brought up in a devoutly religious family, with a rabbi for a grandfather, had turned his back on organised religion and had married my Jewish but non-religious mother, which, in my grandfather's eyes, was almost as bad as marrying a non-Jew.

Fast forward to March 2020 and the onset of Covid. The imposed solitude and feelings of collective dread in those strange times prompted an urge to reclaim something of my heritage and explore my identity. My parents were both dead by this time and the vacuum of lockdown made me long for community and a renewed continuity with the past.

I found a weekly Zoom Hebrew class for beginners run by the Ark Synagogue in Northwood and my sister and I started to attend. There was something very comforting about hearing Hebrew words spoken and explained by Rabbi Aaron. Each letter was discussed and dissected, its meanings explained, along with some of its etymology. Words from my childhood re-emerged, memories were sparked: hearing passages from the Bible read out in halting Hebrew by classmates took me back to those chilly Passover evenings when my father and uncle would fill the living room with a dovetailing of Hebrew prayers and my sister and I would count the hours until liberation!

When I did more research into the letters, I became fascinated by their different layers of meaning and the further I delved into the symbolism of each letter, the more interested I became. I began writing poems in response to each of the 22 Hebrew letters as a way of trying to process the complex feelings aroused by finally learning the language of my forebears. Although I had not had any overarching scheme in mind, these poems seemed to come from the same space within and developed into a cohesive sequence that was as much a playful meditation on language, meaning and sound, as a celebration of the cultural heritage that I grew up within and alongside.

After I had finished the sequence, I realised that it was something that needed to be published as a discrete project and not diluted as part of a larger creative entity. As it was conceived as a homage to my heritage and my family, I also wanted to include some images of the religious objects that had been handed down from my great-grandfather, the rabbi, my grandfather, the disapproving patriarch who'd died before I was born, and my father, who had walked away from organised religion but had never renounced his religious and cultural identity. These are relics of a faith that, for us, may no longer be practised but nonetheless continues to be a crucial part of our identity as Jews.

In these difficult times for people of minority faiths, these poems are intended as an exploration of identity, a paean to the history and origins of an ancient people, a tribute to my family for whom love was more important than blind faith, and an iteration of my commitment to peace and mutual respect between nations.

For my sister, who joined me on this journey.

Aleph Bet

אלף בית

ALEPH BET (ah-lef bate)

Divine sequence, first
consonants sounded
by the world's founder
to banish chaos, words
forging substance—
ocean, stone. Record
of history, sheaves
of fly-wing pages, font
so small each phrase
is a sentence of hardship,
this script is reliquary
and relic: each *ot*, letter,
a sign or wonder rapped
right to left, hammer
and chisel tap-dancing
thought into endurance,
tablet dust a halo rising.
Now these sealed glyphs
with their yield of sense
gaze from the page, black
as the eye of hard faith.
I am become a desert
of wide sand forgetting
every staggered step.

א

ALEPH (ah-lef)

King over breath, mark
of silence in the line,
aleph is mighty, mute.
Shaped from the ox
in the fields, boxy
head, taciturn stare,
it wears its crown
of horns lightly, seals air
in the universe, heat
in the year, lungs
in the body. It's soft,
this god letter, a breeze
kissing the script
it precedes with life.
It splays like the X
marking the spot
where my lips gape
and my tongue cleaves
to the floor of my mouth
as I articulate the *ah*
of the vowel, turning
a crooked figure
into the birth of a word.

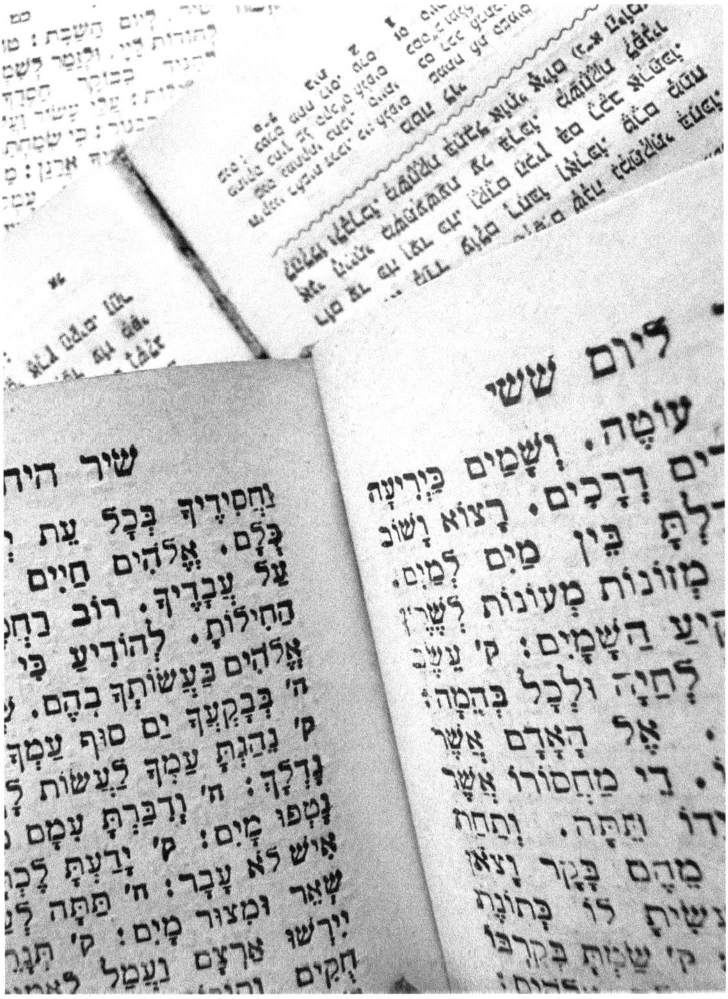
ליום ששי

ב

BET (bate)

Second but not scant,
this letter is a hard kiss
of sound, a pursing of lips
for the telling of the Torah—
in the beginning, *bereshit*.
Shout out for the twos,
heaven and earth, Adam
and Eve, brain and faith,
the birth of this world
and the next. King over
wisdom, they say,
this moulds the mouth
in the soul. I'd say *aba*
for Dad, *ah* like a sigh,
held note high in a song,
the *ba* potent in the silence
and there you have both
sire and subject, loss
and joy. This is the sign,
in shape and meaning,
for a house, its door open,
beckoning always, *barukh*,
brakhah, blessing of family,
friends, laughter, touch.

VI
VII
VIII
IX
X
I
II
III
IV
V

בּ גּ דּ כּ פּ תּ

DAGESH LENE (dah-gesh ley-ney)

Weak only in name, speck
of stress, this dot, black
as a poppy seed, is a stop
on breath in the mouth,
filling the soft centre
of the six *Begadkefat* glyphs
to harden the turbulence
of a purr to plosive push.

ב

VET (vate)

Soft variant of *bet,*
this vacant tent lacks
the emphatic dot
that converts vacuum
to bounty. Voiced mate
of the vehement burr,
vet is a partnering.
that breeds patterns
of contraries, slave
and master, life
and death, gross
and grace. Hewed
in spirit, carved
in voice, this letter
is forced between lip
and teeth, delivering
the vim in words
like *lev*, heart, *avi*,
my dad, *hav*, give, *ahava*,
love. Unlike its twin,
it's ever an end, forever
last and lasting.

ג

GIMMEL (geeh-mel)

In the mouth, palatal,
traced by the voice
as a triangle in the air,
this is three manifest,
two legs and a head
with tripled crown;
soul of balance, symbol
of elemental unity—
air, fire and water—
it's measure and sum
of two and one, *aleph,*
bet, father and son,
holy spirit rising,
On the page, *gimmel*
stands tall, individual
in motion, big foot
ruled by a big heart—
rich as language, king
of wealth, chasing
after the poor with alms.
There is recompense
here, and judgement,
in the echo with g'*mul*,
while the chime of *gamal*
brings in the camel,
neck outstretched
on its desert trek,
its humpback a *gamla*—
ancient bridge between
departure and home.

DAILY PRAYERS
S. ROSENSTEIN

ד

DALET (dah-let)

Fourth, not forthright,
dalet is all deference,
mark of the receivers
of the world, door open
to callers. At the fore,
the first four mothers
of Israel's tribes, four
cups of wine at the *seder*,
four questions posed—
why dip in brine, why
recline, why the *matzo*,
why the *maror* of our past,
flight to freedom, bitter
smack of subjection?
Humble beneficiary,
this stoop is the glyph
of the down-at-heel,
the dispossessed, left
ear cocked for succour,
leg trailing backwards
to a benefactor; lintel
and doorpost, gap sealed
to repel the elements,
sprawl of the living
on tracts of wasteland,
here is the blinking 404
error of existence.
Behind this portal
or sheltered by cloth
crouch the down-and-outs
who are counting on aid.
Which of us will answer
the knock or draw
back the canvas flap?

ה

HEH (hay)

Behold the breath,
its birth at the back
of the tongue, dark
opening to the light
at the seat of swallowing.
This is spirit, soul, sigh,
exhaled in the warmth
of air, cloud on mirror.
Praise its huff before
the last gasp at the end
of words when it serves
as a mother of reading.
Hey, they say, *hallel,*
hallelujah for *Hashem*,
The Name, the creator
of light in an outbreath.
This is the high five
of the body—fingers,
senses, dimensions—
this is the *the*, the *ha*
that deals in specifics,
the spark, the halation
that wakes the wonder.

ו

VAV (vahv)

Divine hook, silver
crook joining curtain
to tabernacle, text
to parchment, clause
to clause as *and*, *vav*
is voiced at the bluff
of teeth on the vertex
of the tongue, its sound
in English veering
toward female parts.
Vehicle of few words
like *vered*, rose, *vey*, woe—
oy vey iz mir wailing
at the pain of living—
this plain Jane of script
is pegged as consonant
and vowel, its dotted *oh*,
o and *ooh* pouting lips
in wonder. Verve
of a thrown spear, view
of man stood very tall,
we're here in the realm
of six, the rule of thumb
for refuge, connection,
the six-winged seraphim
crying *holy*, while trebled
the number will recall
the beast. *Vav* is a vat
of bile, the gallbladder
of the soul, the body's good
and bad conjoined, nail
riveting heaven to earth.

ז

ZAYIN (zah-een)

Hilt and blade thrust
down, digit portrayed,
zayin strikes the drum
for the need to stand
and be counted: seven
for the Sabbath, repose
from the grind, ease
and blessing, it bestows
sustenance. Sourced
from origins that shape
the mattock, its root
is the reap and glean
of crops, food to survive,
mazon or *zun*. Buzzed
with a quiet tongue
between the teeth,
it spells *za'am*, rage,
zman, time, *zicharon*,
memorial, *zacher*,
remember, the *mazel*,
luck, of not being born
there, but here; now,
not then. Kiss the fingers
that graze the *mezuzah*
gracing the door frame
of your house, muzzle
the doubts and uphold
the two-edged weapon
that gains peoples
a home, land, respite.

א ה ח ע ר

GUTTURALS

The low five that gnarr below
the mouth's cavern, *aleph, heh,*
chet, ayin and *resh*, shibboleth
for those with words framed
in the main by tongue and teeth,
these are throat sounds sired
so dark and deep they stop
the flow of speech as they rise.

ח

CHET (khet)

Doorway for the light
falling from on high,
in form this is a fence
against foes, weather.
Magic eight ball telling
of wisdom, grace, *chet*
marks the eighth day
for a new son's cutting
or the miracle of *Chanukah*,
flames alive despite lack
of oil. Rasp hawked up
from the cauldron
of the throat, *kh* brands
the speech of the chosen,
conjuring up the stuff
of youth with *challah*,
Pesach, *chutzpah*, *chuppah*,
the gold *chai* suspended
on its chain beneath
the pulse that churns
adjacent to my trachea,
toasting *l'chaim*, to life.

לי מקדש

ט

TET (tate)

Basket of secrets,
tet, head over tail, rare
in the Torah, teeters
between good, *tov*,
and not. Watch out,
they say, *ha-satan*,
the Evil One, master
of disguise, abets
and misdirects. Cast
down your eyes
before a higher high
and have no truck
with the base snake,
its fate of dust. Hold
fast to the perfect nine,
its strength and truth
a token of authority.
This vessel tends futures
in its uterus—who's sure
what might emerge?
Better perhaps to stay
empty as a kettledrum
nurturing nothing
but dry air and thunder.

י

YOD (yod)

Building block, atom
of consonants, *yod* hangs
in mid-air, common
as a comma, jot-small.
Soul and heart of the Jew—
Yehudi, *Yehudiyyah*, *Yid*—
shaped as a flame
soaring up, yearning
for *Hashem*—pair of *yods*
yoked to evoke *The Name*—
yod is a chute too, tipping
a job lot of blessings
on the yielding few,
Jacob's brood, not *Yok*
or *Yaikultie:* only *frummers*
who swap *good yontifs*
in Yiddish on holy days
and have a yen for ten,
that *minyan* of men
to pray for redemption.
Ten commandments,
ten plagues, ten digits:
yes, *yad* is a hand, a fist,
a pointer, a memorial.
Hear us yell *yada yada*
at the deniers' yammer,
their standing ten count
for the children of *Yisrael*.

ך כּ כ

KAF/KHAF (kaf/khaf)

Spoon, receptacle,
palm cupped, *kaf* carries
the hand's potential—
prayer clasp, pressed
blessing on a head, kiss
of skin in the clinch
of a handshake, clap.
Biform, first of five
to change when final,
it curves in the course
of a word, body bowed,
brow to floor, uncurling
erect as a spike to end
and extend below the line
like the stem of a crotchet,
cadence falling. Why?
Kakha! Because! Dropping
the *dagesh* as if coughing
up the dot like a catch
in the throat to taste
respect, *khavod. Kabed*
et avicha v'et imecha—
honour your father,
your mother, be glad
they succumbed before
the wrench of care, *ke'ev*,
the grief of 2020, *kaf kaf:*
double trouble for a year
of contagion and curse.

ל

LAMED (lah-med)

Lofty majuscule, ladder-
tall, linchpin, kingpin,
King of Kings looming
over its fellows, lording
it between *kes*, throne,
and *malkhoot*, kingdom,
lamed is the large heart,
lev, of this alphabet.
Flying tower, spiritual
might and rule, *aleph*
plus *lamed* make *El*,
the god word, small
name that packs a punch
in a troubled world
where the *lamed-vavniks*,
thirty-six sinless souls,
slave unseen to save us.
Staff and goad, a spur
for learning, it schools
all people to shun evil.
Lingual, elemental,
propelled from the hollow
of the mouth by press
and release of the tongue,
initial *l'* is inseparable
from goal or direction—
'to' or 'for' to progress,
impulse pricking us on.

מ ם

MEM (mem)

Forty, as in the days
and nights of flood,
mem, king over water,
brings cold in the year,
belly in the soul, earth
in the universe. One
of the elemental mothers—
aleph, *mem*, *shin*: air,
water, fire—primordial
mem keeps mum,
clamp of lips at teat,
a murmur of mam,
mummy, *am*, *immi*,
names like mementos
recalling the *mmm*
of comfort and home.
Open as the half moon
of a breaker that looms
at the horizon, it's used
in the middle or to start:
emet, truth, *mikvah*, bath
of rebirth. At the end
of words, it's closed
as the womb, *rachem*,
ministering the *mitzvah*
of umbilical manna
for forty weeks, before
the gush and muscle
of metamorphosis
from the body's muffle.

נ ן

NUN (noon)

Sprouting seed, deceit
embodied by the snake,
seminal *nun* is offspring,
son continuing the line—
though our descent
is uterine, the founding
feminine. Letter fourteen,
like each counted pound
in the stones of puberty,
it's also the inner bull
of wisdom, the coming
of sage years, fifty-fifty
of an ambivalent hand
weighing life's toll,
the unlikely miracle, *nes*,
of happiness. Straight
and open as love, spine
of the heart at the end
of words, *nun* bends
in medial form, echoes
the hunch and fawn
of awe—the drive
to earn a parent's pride,
nachas, that never died.
And *nu*, they'd say, cue
to value the now yet
keep on moving, alive
to the boon of family
in *natan*, past of giving.

ס

SAMECH (sah-mekh)

Circle, shield, unending
succour of an embrace,
samech is bond, wedding
band, sum of equals,
no sadists, no suckers
dead-set on sacrifice.
Sounded with tongue
at rest before the drop
of jaw that signals gasp
or stupor, it brings back
savta, grandma, *saba*,
grandpa, the dark sniff
and snore of sleepovers,
distant trains whistling.
Sayonara to that sanctuary
in Swiss Cottage, freight
of comics, sweeties; *sof*,
end, of sixties clothes,
sixty or so years ago.
No surprise this sign
sits like a sill between
something and nothing,
section versus the whole,
sting of fire one sixtieth
of hell, dreams mere buds
of prophecy, tight sleep
one sixtieth of death.

ע

AYIN (ah-yeen)

Silent sight of body,
the eyes have it, yoked
to a central stem, arrayed
for the story of outside,
the good eye yearning
for *samech* behind, all heart
all hold, evil eye, *ayin hara*,
a slave to sin, hungering
for *peh* ahead, its mouth
a yawn of greed, envy.
Left hand of the soul,
laughter, loss of spleen,
ayin brings in seventy: tally
of words said over wine
to wave the Sabbath in,
ways to classify God, cries
of the narrow-wombed deer
in labour, a life in span
of years. This sign is passive,
silence broken by the yawp
of vowels, tongueless
in their truth. *Ayin* paves
the will's way, angel eye
supping the dazzle, brute
eye guzzling the darkness
of all the light gone bad.

פ פּ

PEH/FEH (pay/fay)

Mouthpiece of insight,
egress for praise, prayer,
or put-down, *peh* is word
of mouth, bringing life
to printed patterns. Pout
of pursed lips, as in *piyyut*,
poem, *panim*, face, *pihuk*
yawn, *peh* has a double, *feh*,
its pair softer, dotless,
for *fonetee*, phonetic, *fehr*,
fair, a ferrying of lips
to upper teeth often
marking foreign loans.
All appetite, *peh* fights
the pull of greed, the *eat*
Dolly eat prompt, prays
for the triumph of good
with Purim's poppy-seed
pastries or *Pesach*'s wine.
Proof of endurance, grey
not past it, *peh* is eighty
like the prophet parting
the sea of reeds. Pumped
with importance, it pays
lip service to the priority
of eyes, feels that worlds
are created by words
that can name the light,
cheeks puffed with pride
at the power of speech.

צ ץ

TSADE (tsah-dee)

Bent fish hook lodged
in the craw of capture,
righteous as the *tsaddik*,
person above misdeed,
tsade is straight-up saintly,
secure from tsk-tsking.
Hiss of a tongue tapping
at the mouth's hard top,
it performs the same task
on its knees, brow to floor,
as erect when last, praise
in upheld arms. *Tsade* ticks
all the boxes for charity,
tsedekah, the less-is-more,
tsimtsum, of self-sacrifice.
Near the end of the line,
this is the sign for ninety,
for sifted saints and mixed
messengers; the arthritic
body becomes a crook
of pain, the stiff curtsies
and bows of its hurts
the outline of praying
as the spirit rises to shine.

●

DAGESH FORTE (dah-gesh for-tey)

Strong as tea poured
from a steel pot, a one-two
punch of sound, this dot
is not particular, points
up almost any letter, makes
it sing with doubled force,
becoming the twinned wings
of a hinge in the word.

ק

QOPH (kof)

Ear of the axe, eye
of heaven's needle,
cramping the stride
of the camel, *qoph*
is an angel voice crying
kadosh, kadosh, kadosh,
thrice holy, crooning
the *Shabbos* prayers,
the Kiddush, quaffing
wine, keeping faith.
But it can be fake,
great mimic, monkey
(*kuf*) see, monkey do,
aping the graceful *heh*
of hallelujahs—left leg
overlong, dunked
below the line, seeking
the profane. Combined
with *resh*, *qoph* counters
life: nothing good comes
from *kar*, cold, polar
opposite of life's breath
or *rek*, empty, hollow
as the heart in death.
And death is here
in this century, this tally
of five scores for a ton.
Say the *Kaddish* then, light
candles in dark rooms
emptier than before
and change base metal
by the alchemy of Law.

ר

RESH (raysh)

Nearing the rear, bad
ringer of *dalet*'s right
angle, reft of its roofing
yod—projecting ear
that might raise
the corrupt to the dais
of heaven—*resh*
is the bowed back
of penury with nought
to its name, naughty
not nice, bankrupt
of faith. Repentance
may yet ring changes
to convert a pauper,
rash, and *rasha*, a rascal,
to *rosh*, head, the skull
a crown, righteous as one
throwing stones. Once
the reign of the upright
is reinstated, manna
might well rain down
on hungry souls stalled
on the world's board,
unable to pass go/collect
two hundred *zuzim*. All
of us deserve a chance
to turn things round
from rough to comfort,
however near the end—
bereshit, in the beginning,
the word, the response,
the response, the word.

שׁ/שׂ

SHIN (sheen/seen)

Trident of flames,
king over fire, sear
and smelt to transform
and refine, *shin* gives
three times one hundred
percent for divine sway,
redress, the shimmy
from falsehood to truth.
This is change for good—
shush of the sunk tongue
to still the charm and chat
of *shedim*, vile demons
asquat the shoulder, dot
on the left, *S* for sin,
on the right, *Sh* for shine.
Sign of the *Shaddai*—
the Almighty—scribed
on the *mezuzah's* slant
sheath, this crown of lines
starts the prayer within,
Shema Yisrael—Hear,
O Israel—praise
the one. *Shin* blesses,
fingers split like Spock
for a tripartite salute
of truce, *Shalom*
Aleichem, shoring up
its stellar spinoffs
live long and prosper,
peace and long life.

ת

TAV (tav)

Omen or seal, tail
of this train of thoughts,
tav is a tag for the end
of the line, the terminal.
Badge of life, of death,
traced on foreheads
in blood or sinless ink
before the holy temple
fell, *tav*'s twin theme
toes the line—numbers
never lie—four hundred
to typify the world's levels
of evil, sparks of god
soul, a total to transform
all negatives to good.
Token of truth, *emet*
—*aleph, mem, tav,* start,
middle, end of the *Aleph Bet*—
enlightenment attained
through the letters' trek,
tav has been long awaited,
hard-earned. It is the sign
that tips us into a perfect state,
the question's answer, *teshuva*,
repentance and return.

□

UNKNOWN

consonant that awaits
revelation in a later world,
this is the missing shape
that will mend the place
of hurt where grief plumes
like a city of debris rent
with sirens. Creator
of new words that turn
wrong to right, repair,
reform, this letter
once heard will chime
its rightness. Enigma
of tongue against palate
or lips kissing breath,
it will rise in thanksgiving
from our depths and press
its utterance to the cheek
of the child who sleeps
through the night's silence.

Notes

אלף בית

The Hebrew alphabet consists of 22 letters, all consonants, none of which are lowercase. Each letter has its own sound, numeric value and a plethora of mystical and symbolic connotations.

א

Numeric value is one, alluding to the oneness of God.
The original pictograph represents an ox, and therefore strength.
A number of the divine names begin with *aleph*.

בּ and ב

Numeric value is 2.
The pictograph is a house or dwelling.

Dagesh lene (*kal*)
Diacritic that takes the form of a dot, appearing in six letters (*bet, gimmel, dalet, kaf, peh, tav*) known by the acronym *Begadkefat*. The dot gives these letters a harder pronunciation.

ג

Numeric value is 3.
The pictograph is a camel.
In the Talmud, it is said that *gimmel* symbolizes a man running after a poor man (the next letter, *dalet*) to give him charity.
The word g'*mul* means recompense or benefit.

ד

Numeric value is 4.
The pictograph resembles a closed (hanging) tent door.
The word *dalet* (door) comes from *dalah*, which means to impoverish and the word *dalut* means poor or impoverished.

ה

Numeric value is 5.
The meaning of *heh* is to look or behold.
The letter functions as the definite article in Hebrew and also denotes the feminine at the end of a word.
Although the original Hebrew alphabet consisted only of consonants,

certain letters (*aleph*, *hey*, *vav*, *yod*) gradually also became used to indicate vowels and are known as 'mothers of reading'(*matres lectionis* in Latin) when used in this function.

ו

Numeric value is 6.
The pictograph resembles a tent peg.
The meaning of the word *vav* is hook.
The letter can represent the word 'and'.

ז

Numeric value is 7.
The pictograph resembles a sword.
The word *zayin* means weapon or sword.
Mezuzah: a piece of parchment inscribed with specific Hebrew verses from the Torah, which Jews affix in a small case to the doorposts of their home.

אהחצר

These five guttural letters are created in the throat. They interrupt the normal flow of speech due to the movement of tongue and throat necessary for correct pronunciation.

ח

Numeric value is 8.
The pictograph resembles a wall or fence.
The *Chanukah* miracle occurred during the Maccabean revolt and describes the finding of a jug of pure oil that was only enough to light the lamp for one day, but actually lasted for the full eight days.
Challah: braided bread eaten typically on special occasions.
Chuppah: wedding canopy.

ט

Numeric value is 9.
The pictograph resembles a snake curled inside a basket.

י

Numeric value is 10.
The pictograph resembles an arm or a hand and the word *yod* means arm or hand.

Yod is used to form all the other letters and, as such, indicates God's omnipresence.
Frummer: a Jew who is devout, from the Yiddish for *pious one*.
Good Yontif: a Yiddish phrase to wish others a 'good holiday'.
Minyan: the quorum required for Jewish communal worship.

ך כּ כ
Numeric value is 20.
The pictograph resembles the palm of a hand.
The word *kaf* means palm or spoon. It comes from the root word *kafah* meaning to bend or bow down.
With a *dagesh*, it is pronounced *kaf*, and without, it is the softer version *khaf*. It is one of five *sofit* letters that change to a closed form at the end of the word.

ל
Numeric value is 30.
The pictograph resembles a shepherd's staff or goad.
It is the tallest letter, being the only one that rises above the top line.
As the 12th letter, it is regarded as one of the central letters or heart of the alphabet.
The original meaning of *lamed* was to incite or goad and its root is *lamad* meaning to learn or teach.
The letter *lamed* is also used as a prefix, meaning 'towards' or 'for'.
Lamed-vavniks: 36 hidden righteous people who wander the earth unknown to each other doing good deeds. As the legend goes, as long as they exist, the wrath of God is kept at bay.

ם מ
Numeric value is 40.
The pictograph resembles a wave of water. It has several related meanings: water, nations and languages. It also represents the womb, as water is the womb of creation.
It is one of five *sofit* letters that change to a closed form at the end of the word.

ן נ
Numeric value is 50.
The pictograph resembles a seed, and is believed to be derived from an Egyptian hieroglyph of a snake.

Nun can mean deceit or miracle, among other things.
It is one of five *sofit* letters that change to a closed form at the end of the word.

ס
Numeric value is 60.
The pictograph resembles a shield or a circle without beginning or end.
The root of the word *samekh* means to support.

ע
Numeric value is 70.
The pictograph loosely resembles an eye, or two eyes connected to a common optic nerve.
The word *ayin* means eyes, to see, and by extension to understand and obey.
Like *aleph*, it is a silent letter and it is said that *ayin* sees but does not speak.

פ פּ
Numeric value is 80.
The pictograph resembles a mouth and the word *peh* means mouth.
Peh has a medial form and a *sofit* form.
With a *dagesh* (dot), it is pronounced as a hard 'p', without a *dagesh*, it has the softer 'ph' sound for *feh*.

ץ צ
Numeric value is 90.
The pictograph resembles a man on his side, representing need. It derives its name from the shape of a fishing hook and is related to the root *tzod*, meaning to hunt or capture.
Tsade has a medial form and a *sofit* form.

Dagesh forte (*chazak*)
This dot indicates that a letter has been doubled and can be used with any Hebrew consonant except for the guttural letters.

ק
Numeric value is 100.
The origin of the shape of this letter is unclear and may have

depicted the eye of a needle or the back of the head. It may also have depicted the sun on the horizon.

The meaning of *kof* or *kuf* is monkey.

Qoph is associated with holiness being the first letter of the word *kadosh* meaning holy. However, it is the only letter that extends below the baseline, representing one who ventures below the acceptable, and is thus also associated with impure spiritual forces or evil.

ר

Numeric value is 200.

The design of the *resh* represents someone bent over, a poor person, similar to *dalet*.

A poor person is permitted to collect charity from a synagogue if they do not possess 200 *zuzim*, which is the threshold above which an individual is no longer poor. The poverty of *resh* is more wretched than the destitution of *dalet*.

The meaning of *resh* is poor, evil or head.

שׁ/שׂ

Numeric value is 300.

This letter has a 'sh' sound if the dot is on the upper right, and an 's' sound if the dot is on the upper left.

Shin has various meanings: tooth, steadfast, change, return, year.

Its three prongs can be seen to symbolize flames.

ת

Numeric value is 400.

The pictograph depicts a mark, sign, omen or seal.

It is the symbol of truth, perfection and completion.

It can signify both life, *ticheyeh*, or death, *tamut*. Its *gematria* shares this dichotomy, representing good as in the 400 sparks of godliness versus the 400 levels of evil.

□

According to a 13th-century Kabbalistic text, there is a letter missing from the present-day alphabet and this letter will be revealed only in the future. Every defect in our universe is mysteriously connected with this letter and when it is revealed, it will right all wrongs.

Photos

Page 13. Pages from inherited prayer books.

Page 15. The ornate inlaid cover of a prayer book which belonged to my great-grandfather, the rabbi (detail).

Page 19. Prayer book belonging to my grandfather, who changed the family name from Rosenstein to Rose on coming to this country.

Page 22. My father's prayer shawl (detail).

Page 27. The menorah that used to stand beside our Christmas tree in the lounge (detail).

Page 30. A silver pendant with the 72 names of God bought on my first trip to Israel in 2019.

Page 33. My father's *kappel* or skull cap.

Page 36. My gold *chai* necklace, bought for me by my parents when I was in my early teens.

Page 40. The cover of my father's *haggadah* (book telling the story of the Exodus used at *Pesach*).

Page 44. The velvet bags containing my father's prayer shawl and prayer box (detail).

Page 48. My father's *tefillah* or prayer box (detail).

www.ingramcontent.com/pod-product-compliance
Ingram Content Group UK Ltd.
Pitfield, Milton Keynes, MK11 3LW, UK
UKHW041618260825
462269UK00002B/46